21ST
CENTURY
DEBATES

WASTE, RECYCLING, AND REUSE

OUR IMPACT ON THE PLANET

ROB BOWDEN

RAINTREE
STECK-VAUGHN
RSVP PUBLISHERS

A Harcourt Company

Austin   New York
www.raintreesteckvaughn.com

21st Century Debates Series

Climate Change	Energy Resources	Genetics	Internet
Media	Rain Forests	Surveillance	Waste, Recycling, and Reuse

Published by Raintree Steck-Vaughn Publishers, an imprint of the Steck-Vaughn Company

Library of Congress Cataloging-in-Publication Data
Bowden, Rob
    Waste, recycling, and reuse : our impact on the planet/Rob Bowden.
        p. cm—(21st century debates)
    Includes bibliographical references and index.
    ISBN 0-7398-3180-1   ISBN 978-0-7398-3180-9
        1. Refuse and refuse disposal—Juvenile literature. 2. Recycling (Waste, etc.)—Juvenile literature.
[1. Refuse and refuse disposal. 2.Recycling(Waste)] I. Title. II. Series.

TD792 .B69 2001
363.72'8—dc21

00-054294

Printed and bound in China
3 4 5 6 7 8 9 LB 11 10 09 08 07

This book used information gathered from a wide range of sources, but the author would like to acknowledge the Waste Watch website and a Channel 4 television documentary series entitled "Against Nature" as particularly useful sources of facts and viewpoints. Material provided by Friends of the Earth (UK) and the Warmer Bulletin of the World Resources Foundation was also very useful.

Picture acknowledgments: Rob Bowden 12, 13, 42, 46; Ecoscene 6 (Amanda Gazidis), 9 (Rosemary Greenwood), 41 (Chinch Gryniewicz), 53 (Eva Messler), 55 (Andy Binns), 58 (Peter Hulme); HWPL 33 (Gordon D. R. Clements); Forlaget Flachs/Ole Steen Hansen 17, 45, 49; Robert Harding 14 (David Lomax), 28 & cover foreground; Panos Pictures 10 (Jeremy Hartley), 20 (Liba Taylor), 21 (Sean Spague), 34 (Giacomo Pirozzi), 39 (Chris Stower), 43 (Jeremy Hartley), 48 (Jeremy Hartley), 59 (Chris Stower); Photodisc Inc. 54; Splash International 56; Still Pictures 4 (Francisco Marque), 5 (Shehzad Noorani), 11 (Jean-Leo Dugast), 16 (top/Jim Wark), 16 (bottom/Mark Edwards), 18 (Mark Edwards), 19 (Mark Edwards), 22 & cover background (David Drain), 24 (Ray Pfortner), 31 (Gerard & Margi Moss), 32 (Nigel Dickinson), 35 (Julio Etchart), 36 (Mark Edwards), 37 (Dominique Halleux), 38 (Ray Pfortner), 40 (Hartmut Schwartzbach), 51 (Mark Edwards), 57 (Jorgen Schytte); White-Thomson Publishing 7.

Cover: Foreground picture shows staff undergoing specialist training for handling hazardous wastes; background picture shows a landfill site where much of our waste is buried with little thought about the consequences or alternatives.

CONTENTS

THE WASTE DEBATE

What Is Waste?

Nature has recycled its wastes for millions of years: As this fallen tree rots, it becomes a food source for new plants and animals.

Waste is the material remaining at the end of a process. It is the material that is not used or is thrown away because it has no further use, like the bottle after you have finished a drink or the grass cuttings when you mow the lawn.

All life produces waste, but the amount and type of waste produced varies greatly. Some wastes are harmful, while others are vital resources, without which life could not survive. Trees, for example, produce oxygen as a waste gas, which humans and other life forms need to breathe. Today, humans produce most of the world's waste—and as our knowledge of science and technology increases, and we continue to develop processes that exploit natural resources for our own benefit, the amount of waste we produce may also increase.

Types of waste

The main types of waste we produce are municipal (MSW), industrial, hazardous, and human. Municipal waste comes from our homes, schools, stores, and offices and includes left-over food and the packaging and products we throw away. Industrial waste comes from factories and power plants and is mainly made up of the waste materials, liquids, and gases from production processes. Hazardous waste includes chemical, toxic, and radioactive waste and comes mainly from industry and agriculture. These wastes are of special concern because they can be extremely dangerous to both people and the environment. And with the world's population now over six billion people, and still growing, waste from our own bodies is becoming a problem, too.

A Bangladeshi woman searches through the local Municipal Solid Waste (MSW) at a garbage dump in Dhaka for useful materials. Many of the things we throw away could be used by others.

The waste problem

The problem with waste is that it remains in our environment—we move waste from one place to another but rarely get rid of it completely. Nature has recycled waste material for millions of years as part of the global ecosystem, but human numbers increased so rapidly during the last century that the environment is now threatened by our activities and the wastes these produce. This damage can already be seen in the contamination of rivers, the poisoning of soils, and the polluted air in many of our towns and cities.

Many scientists believe that if we don't act soon, both to reduce waste and to use resources more carefully, the global ecosystem will fail, with the result that many species, including humans, could

FACT

In one year there is enough waste produced in the United States to fill garbage cans that would stretch from the Earth to the moon.

VIEWPOINT

"There are not enough resources in this world to have living standards at the same level as in the United States for every single person in this world."
Lisa Jordan, Director, Bank Information Center

become endangered. But resources are needed for economic growth and development to provide food, housing, and jobs. This is particularly important in developing countries where many people live in poverty and need economic development to help improve their standard of living. However, if these people are to live like those in developed countries, they will use more resources and produce more waste.

Sustainable development

Some scientists now believe that it is possible to have economic growth while reducing waste at the same time. They use the term "sustainable development" to describe this. It means that we have to think carefully about how we use resources today, so that we do not use them all up or harm the environment for future generations. Those who believe in sustainable development tell us that this is only possible if we all make changes now in the way we live.

Many people take some of their waste to special collection places, such as this scrap recycling center.

Reduction, reuse, and recovery

One of the easiest changes we can make to the way we live is to think about the three Rs—Reduction, Reuse, and Recovery. We can reduce our use of

resources by turning off a running water tap, or by improving production processes in factories. We can reuse containers and packaging for other purposes, or use the same product several times (like a returnable drink bottle). We can recover materials such as glass, paper, and metals (like aluminum drink cans and steel from old cars) for recycling. Together, the three Rs could make a huge difference in our use of resources and the wastes we produce, but making the necessary changes is not as simple as it sounds.

These bicycles in Copenhagen, Denmark, are part of a city cycle network that encourages people to use bicycles instead of cars. Cycling is a form of sustainable transportation that produces very little waste.

To understand the problem fully, it is necessary to examine the history, nature, and management of waste and look at its impact on people and environments around the world. We need to question whether sustainable development is possible, and to look at the technology and ideas that it might involve. We also need to consider what we can do in our own lives and take a look at what our own future might be like.

DEBATE

Before you read further, think about what you already know about waste and recycling. Where does waste come from? How is it handled? What harm can it cause? What can we do about it? It might be worth making a list of your ideas and seeing how many of them come up in the rest of the book.

WORLD OF WASTE

Waste or Resource?

Many people think that we now live in a world of waste where pollution and environmental destruction are unavoidable. They argue that there are too many people using too many resources and that the planet cannot cope. But not all people use the planet's resources equally, and some are more affected by waste than others. In fact, what is considered waste by some people may be an important resource to others.

Historical waste

Human activity has always produced waste of some kind, and this has been very useful in helping us understand how our ancestors used to live. Archaeology, the science used to study our past, often relies on materials such as pottery, tools, jewelry, and clothing that were lost or thrown away hundreds, or even thousands, of years ago. It is through examining these wastes that we now understand more about previous civilizations, like the Egyptians. Nature also leaves wastes, such as fossils, which show us what plant and animal life were like in the past. Some of the most famous fossils are those of the dinosaurs that roamed the Earth between 225 and 65 million years ago.

Growing waste!

Today, humans are producing more and more waste. Our growing numbers and changing lifestyles mean we use greater quantities of the resources around us. Population growth in the last century was very rapid, rising from just 1.65 billion people in 1900 to over 6 billion in the year 2000. Although the rate

City streets, like this one in New York City, are examples of modern consumer lifestyles. Much of what we buy is thrown away almost immediately, creating piles of waste.

of growth has now slowed down, we are still increasing by 78 million people every year, which is more than the populations of Denmark, Sweden, Finland, Norway, the Netherlands, Belgium, Switzerland, Hungary, and Austria combined. Some scientists believe our numbers could double again by the year 2200, but most think that the world population will stabilize at about 10 billion people. Whatever the numbers, population growth places an ever greater pressure on natural resources. We use more and more to provide ourselves with food and goods, and in turn, create more waste.

The types of waste we produce have changed over the years. Two hundred years ago, most of the wastes we produced were made of natural products that the environment was able to decompose or recycle. However, the Industrial Revolution at the end of the 18th century led to the exploitation of fossil fuels and other resources that have since been used to make synthetic products. These can be seen all around us, from the plastic packaging of foods to the human-made fibers in the clothes we wear. Other examples are the fuel we burn in our vehicles and the paints we use in our homes. All of these products create wastes both during their production and after they have been used. The problem with these new wastes is that many of them do not decompose easily, so we have to think carefully about how we dispose of them.

Distribution of waste

Although waste is a global concern, not all countries produce equal quantities of waste. In general it is the more developed and industrialized countries that produce the most. The United States alone (which has less than 5 percent of the world's population) is responsible for an estimated 19 percent of the world's domestic waste. The types of waste produced also vary from country to country. In developed countries a large proportion of waste includes human-made products such as chemicals, plastics, and metals. In developing countries more of the waste is organic, and can therefore be safely composted, but this situation is changing as these countries develop. In many African nations, for example, plastic bags are becoming a major waste problem, because they replace the traditional baskets made from natural materials.

In developing countries, such as here in Burkina Faso, much of what people eat and use comes from their natural surroundings, and most of their wastes are biodegradable.

The increasing number of motor vehicles on our roads has led many cities, such as Bangkok in Thailand, to suffer from heavily polluted air caused by waste exhaust gases.

This map of carbon dioxide emissions for different parts of the world shows that not all countries produce equal amounts of waste.

One indicator of global inequalities in waste production is carbon dioxide emissions. Carbon dioxide is a waste gas produced when we burn fossil fuels to power vehicles, provide energy, and produce manufactured goods. The map on this page shows that North American people are by far the biggest producers of carbon dioxide, each one producing over twice as much as a European and 18 times the amount of a person in Africa.

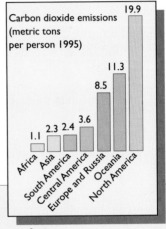

Carbon dioxide emissions (metric tons per person 1995)

Africa	Asia	South America	Central America	Europe and Russia	Oceania	North America
1.1	2.3	2.4	3.6	8.5	11.3	19.9

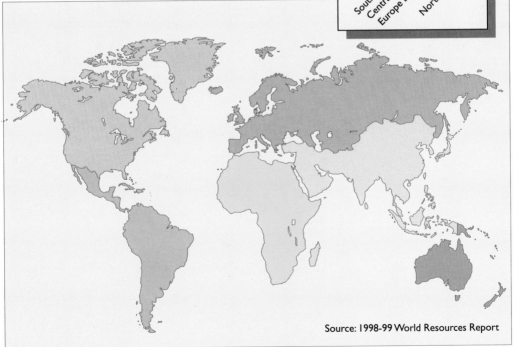

Source: 1998-99 World Resources Report

Waste or resource?

It is important to realize that what one person considers waste, another might consider an important resource. By looking at an East African market, for example, it is possible to see how people make use of materials that many would consider trash. Plastic bottles are cleaned and resold for holding cooking oil, water, milk, or other liquids. Old food cans are collected and made into kerosene lamps, and oil drums are cut up and used to make small stoves called "jikos." Old tires can be made into sandals and the inner tubes cut up to make strong ties for holding goods onto bicycles or for tying things together. Very little is wasted, not even food scraps, which are fed to goats, sheep, and cattle waiting to be sold.

In developing countries, where raw materials can be very expensive, waste is sometimes used as a resource. This man sells lanterns and stoves made of old food cans and oil drums at a market in Jinja, Uganda.

In Asia whole communities have developed out of the waste industry. Over 60,000 people live and work on waste dumps in the Philippines' capital, Manila. Although forced to scavenge to earn a living, such communities perform an important job, and in developing countries it has been estimated that they handle up to 75 percent of urban waste. In Bangalore, India, it has been estimated that waste pickers collect and process some 500 tons of waste every day, compared to just 37 tons collected by the municipal workers.

Industrialized nations do use some wastes as resources, but this normally involves some form of industrial remanufacture rather than direct use. One example of this is the reuse of plastic drink bottles, which are melted down and then spun into a special insulating fiber used in making sleeping bags and fleece jackets.

Unmanaged waste like this, by the side of a road in Uganda, is a major problem in many countries and can attract vermin, such as rats and birds, that spread diseases.

DEBATE

How important do you think population growth is to the waste problems we have? In which part of the world do you think population growth could be particularly troublesome, and why?

TYPES
OF WASTE

Waste from Where?

It is possible to think about waste in many ways, such as its form (solid, liquid, or gas), how dangerous it is (safe, low risk, or hazardous), and how it is disposed of (buried, burned, or diluted). This means it can be very difficult to compare waste in one region with that of another. However, one way to do this is to look at the different sources of wastes and at how they are produced.

Municipal Solid Waste (MSW)

Street collections like this one in São Paulo, Brazil, help to keep our homes free from trash.

Municipal solid waste is the waste generated by a municipality (a town or district). It includes household or domestic trash, often stored in garbage cans for a weekly street collection; the waste produced by stores, offices, restaurants, schools, and hospitals; and that collected from public waste bins. Larger "bulk" items, such as old appliances and furniture, and even grass and plant cuttings from gardens and parks, are also counted as MSW.

Paper and paper products such as cardboard packaging dominate the MSW produced in most developed countries, but in many developing countries vegetable matter is the greatest item. The chart opposite compares the composition of MSW in the

United States (a rich developed country) and Uganda (a poor developing country). How do the figures compare with what you throw away?

Municipal solid waste is often only a small part (less than 10 percent) of the waste produced in a country, but this does not account for the entire "life cycle" of the product. In the UK, for example, it is estimated that for every ton of household waste another 25 tons of waste has already been generated.

Industrial waste

Among the biggest producers of industrial waste are mines, which create large quantities of waste material called tailings. When mining for copper, bauxite, lead, and tin, over 75 percent of the excavated material ends up as tailings, and in the case of gold, the figure is 99.99 percent. Some mining processes also use large volumes of chemicals or liquids, which add to the waste generated and can often be toxic or hazardous. For example, in the Amazon region of South America mercury is used to separate gold from gravel, and to extract around 100 tons of gold, at least 130 tons of toxic mercury are released into the environment.

FACT

The amount of waste generated by the United States every day is more than twice the weight of the entire population.

VIEWPOINT

"If everybody in the world was to consume like the British, the Europeans, or the Americans then we'd need about eight planets to meet people's needs and it would still be unsustainable."
Tony Juniper, Campaigns Manager, Friends of the Earth

Composition of MSW—United States and Uganda
(as percent of total)

Material	U. S.	Uganda
Paper	40	5.4
Metals	9	3.1
Plastics	8	1.6
Glass	7	0.9
Trimmings/cuttings	18	8.0
Food/Vegetable Matter	7	73.8
Others	11	7.2

Sources: Government of Uganda and U.S. Environmental Protection Agency

The red color of this lake in Michigan, was caused by tailings and effluent from an iron-ore mine. Not all wastes are so visible.

Industries making products like paper, leather, aluminum, steel, and textiles also use large quantities of water. One pound of paper, for example, uses about 26 gallons (100 l) of water, whereas to make one pound of suit cloth requires over 710 gallons (2,700 l) of water. This demand for water explains why many industrial plants are located close to rivers, but rivers also receive waste water that is normally discharged as effluent after the manufacturing process. This presents a problem when the waste water contains chemicals and sediment left over from production processes. Rivers such as the Rhine in Western Europe are heavily polluted with chemicals such as lead, mercury, and arsenic from the industries along its banks, and this is the same river that has to supply drinking water for over 20 million people.

Industry also uses a great deal of energy, which itself produces waste gases and other materials when it is generated. Sulfur dioxide and nitric oxides emitted

FACT

When Mount Pinatubo in the Philippines erupted in 1991 it released about 30 million tons of sulfur dioxide in a few hours. This is almost twice as much as that emitted by all the factories, power plants, and cars in the United states in a whole year.

Coal-fired power plants produce very visible wastes, but some scientists now believe that other sources, such as motor vehicles, are more responsible for waste gases.

from power plants have attracted particular attention because of their link with acid rain (see page 30, The Costs of Waste), but vehicles, industry, and natural occurrences, such as volcanic eruptions, are said to be just as responsible.

The problem with industry is that, even though it produces large quantities of waste, manufacturing is necessary for economic growth and development. It was the Industrial Revolution that gave many of us the high standards of living we enjoy today, and in developing countries many consider industrial development to be the answer to reducing poverty. There are instances of industrial inventions that can solve their own waste problems, such as the ability to recycle certain materials that also help to improve the environment. But industrial waste still remains a major concern, and there is a lot more that could be done.

Hazardous waste

Certain wastes are classified as hazardous when they pose a serious threat to human health and the environment. These wastes normally come from

This Danish power plant has been made cleaner by converting from coal to natural gas. It now emits 75 percent less carbon dioxide and uses its waste heat to provide hot water for local residents.

VIEWPOINTS

"Extensive pesticide use is a symptom of an agricultural system that is no longer about food or people, the land or the environment, but just about profits."
Nikki van der Gaag.
New Internationalist.
May 2000

"Without pesticides and fertilizers, U.S. farm exports would fall to zero...and millions of people around the world would starve."
U.S. Agricultural Retailers Association in
New Internationalist.
May 2000

Much of the pesticide sprayed on these Italian peaches falls onto the soil as waste and enters the local water supply.

industrial processes and products, but they also include chemicals used in modern agriculture and medical waste from hospitals. The use of chemicals increased dramatically in the last century with production rising from one million tons in 1930 to over 500 million tons by 1990. About 80,000 chemicals are in regular use, and in addition to many being harmful in themselves they often produce further hazardous wastes during their manufacture. If allowed into the environment, hazardous wastes can contaminate soils, pollute water, and enter the food chain, harming plants, animals, and people. In 1962 Rachel Carson wrote a famous book called *Silent Spring* about the dangers of an agricultural pesticide called DDT entering the food chain. Her book shocked the public and made them aware that hazardous wastes could build up in the environment. DDT was eventually banned in many countries, but is still used in some developing areas. Today most hazardous wastes can be treated or destroyed to make them harmless, but old disposal sites still pose a threat, and new materials are being created every day, many of which could be hazardous in the future.

Radioactive waste

Radioactive wastes are the most hazardous of all. They need to be handled very carefully, since they can remain dangerous for thousands of years. There are three levels of radioactive waste. Low level waste comes from institutions using radioactive technology, such as X-ray machines in hospitals and airports.

Some believe nuclear energy is safe if the radioactive waste is handled properly. Here, used fuel rods are being loaded into special transport containers at a nuclear plant in Germany.

Intermediate level waste comes mainly from the nuclear energy industry and includes the substances used in cooling and storing nuclear fuel. High level radioactive waste includes used nuclear fuel from reactors in power plants and submarines. Although it is present only in small quantities, it remains extremely harmful to human health for many years, which is why it is so hazardous. Nuclear fuel can be reprocessed at specialist sites, such as Cap de la Hague in France, but this process produces additional quantities of low, intermediate, and high level radioactive waste, some of which must be kept safe for 250,000 years. If radioactive waste can be safely stored, then some believe nuclear power could be a solution to our energy needs. This is because it does not produce the greenhouse gases released when fossil fuels are burned. However, concerns about safety, after accidents such as that at Chernobyl in 1986, have caused many countries to stop building nuclear plants.

Human waste

Each person produces an average of .3 gallons (1.2 l) of urine and 7 ounces (200 g) of feces per day as waste products of their digestive system. These contain harmful viruses that can cause serious diseases such as diarrhea, cholera, and hepatitis,

In many developing countries, the lack of sewers means that human waste is released untreated into local rivers. This latrine is in a slum area of Dhaka, Bangladesh.

if they are not disposed of carefully. In most developed nations, human waste is collected in sewage systems and carried away by water in underground pipes to special treatment plants. These remove most of the viruses and make the sewage safer for disposal into rivers or the ocean. Not all human waste is treated, however, and in parts of the UK over 50 percent of sewage is released straight into the ocean. People using the ocean for recreation have formed action groups such as Surfers Against Sewage to encourage better treatment of sewage before it is released. Sewage can also be used as a fertilizer for agricultural use since it is biodegradable. But there is a problem with this, because sewage often contains chemicals from industry and soaps used for laundry and bathing, which are collected in the same pipe systems. These chemicals raise the cost of treatment and can make the treated sewage unsuitable for use as a fertilizer.

VIEWPOINT

"The best thing that could happen to those countries [Third World] is to industrialize rapidly and have their economies grow so they have the resources not only to be healthier, but also to protect their environment."
Steve Hayward, Director, Pacific Research Center

In rural areas of China, human waste is collected in buckets and emptied onto the fields each morning as a natural fertilizer to encourage crop growth.

In developing countries sewage systems are rare, even in large cities such as Jakarta in Indonesia, which with over ten million inhabitants has no sewage system for collecting human waste. Uncollected or untreated human wastes like this can cause major health problems that are among the world's biggest killers.

DEBATE

All wastes can cause problems, but if we are concerned with limiting their impact, which type do you think we should focus on as a priority, and why?

DISPOSAL OF WASTES

Out of Sight, Out of Mind?

Every time you put garbage in a trash can, wash yourself, or travel in a vehicle, you are creating wastes, but how often do you stop to think about where they go? Public awareness of the potential dangers of waste is increasing, however, and waste disposal is now a big industry employing many thousands of people. But the options for waste disposal are limited, because the main disposal routes are onto the land, into the air, or into water, although some countries even trade waste.

Huge landfill sites, like this one in the UK, bury thousands of tons of waste every day, but many believe these sites will become a waste problem for future generations.

Onto the land

Much of the world's solid waste is simply dumped onto vacant land and left to decompose or be covered by further waste and dust or soil. This is particularly so in developing countries, where large mountains of waste can be seen close to centers of population, like Nairobi in Kenya, or Manila in the Philippines.

DISPOSAL OF WASTES

A safer form of disposal is to bury waste in landfill sites, such as old quarries and mines or specially excavated sites. The waste is normally compacted with bulldozers and covered with soil at the end of each day. This prevents pests such as flies and rats, which spread diseases, scavenging for scraps. Once the site is completely full, the waste is covered with more soil and left to decompose over time. Covered landfill sites can then be landscaped to provide recreation facilities, such as golf courses, or low-cost building land for industry and retail estates.

As waste decomposes it produces large quantities of methane gas. This is highly explosive if not managed properly, and it is also a major greenhouse gas. An estimated 1,400 landfill sites in the UK were at risk from methane explosions in 1989, and in 1986 one such explosion destroyed a nearby home. Properly controlled, however, methane can be collected and burned as a fuel to generate electricity. In Canada, landfills generate over one million tons of methane per year, which is equivalent to nine million barrels of oil and enough to heat 500,000 homes. In 1998 only 25 percent of this gas was captured, but even this caused a reduction in Canada's greenhouse gases equivalent to removing 1.6 million cars from the roads.

FACT

Cows and termites are said to produce more methane than landfill sites as a by-product of their digestive systems.

Landfill sites can provide cheap land for recreation facilities or industrial and retail sites, but only if the explosive methane gas is properly vented.

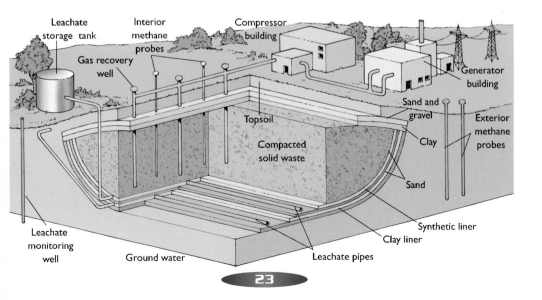

Leachate storage tank · Interior methane probes · Compressor building · Gas recovery well · Generator building · Topsoil · Sand and gravel · Exterior methane probes · Compacted solid waste · Clay · Sand · Leachate monitoring well · Ground water · Leachate pipes · Clay liner · Synthetic liner

This paper mill in New York State emits a lot of waste directly into the air. Manufacturing paper using recycled instead of raw materials would reduce air pollution by 74 percent.

Leachate is associated with landfill sites. It is formed when chemicals and heavy metals dissolve in rainwater, which can then leak into local water and soils. In 1978 the "Love Canal" landfill in New York began leaking toxic and carcinogenic leachate from waste buried 40 years earlier, causing a school and housing estate that had been built on it to be evacuated. Special linings are put around modern landfill sites to control leachate (see diagram on page 23), and hazardous waste is increasingly limited to special containment sites. In France, containment sites have linings at least 16 feet (5 m) thick, but even these have experienced leakages due to damage by chemicals in the leachate.

Into the air

Large volumes of gases and particles are emitted into the air by vehicles, factories, homes, and power plants. You can often see and smell these wastes, such as the smoke from chimneys and fumes from vehicle exhausts. Because of their links with acid rain and our fears of global warming, they have been the focus of actions to control waste in recent years. Emissions of carbon dioxide (CO_2) associated with fossil fuels have been particularly targeted.

Despite concern over air emissions, many countries are building high temperature incinerators to burn waste instead of burying it in landfills. These

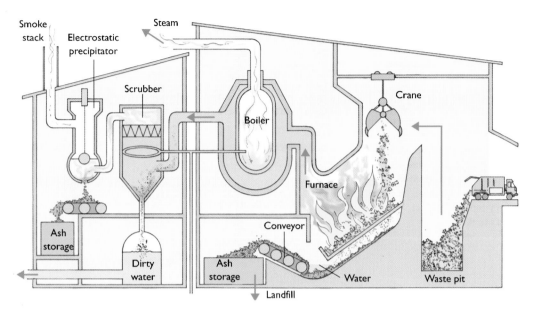

incinerators are said to reduce the bulk of waste by up to 90 percent and to remove 99.99 percent of all toxic materials. But they require careful management and expensive technology to keep temperatures at over 2,190°F (1,200°C) if toxic compounds such as PCBs are to be fully destroyed. Partially burned PCBs emit dioxins that can cause cancer and birth defects, and have been described as "the most toxic man-made chemical ever produced."

Even efficient incinerators produce their own wastes in the form of ash and gases. The ash can often be extremely hazardous due to the high concentrations of metals such as lead and cadmium, and must be carefully handled. Waste gases include nitrous oxides and sulfur dioxide, but these can be prevented from entering the atmosphere by using "scrubbers" in the chimney stacks. Scrubbers act like giant sponges, absorbing waste gases in a liquid that is then disposed of as slurry. Carbon dioxide is still emitted, but this is less damaging to the atmosphere than the methane that would be released if the waste was buried.

Incinerators reduce waste and can generate energy, but there are concerns about their safety.

VIEWPOINTS

"State-of-the-art incineration systems are always outfitted with modern scrubbers. It has been proven that the air leaving a new incineration facility is cleaner than the air we breathe in."
Eco-Waste Solutions, Canada

"...scrubbing systems don't 'clean' incinerators, they simply give you a choice of what you want to pollute; the air, or the soil/groundwater."
Phil Davis, Birmingham Friends of the Earth, UK

FACT

In the United States over the past 25 years, the population has increased by 30 percent, the number of cars by over 100 percent, and the economy by over 100 percent, but emissions of the six main air pollutants have decreased by 30 percent.

Sometimes the heat from the burning process in the incinerators is used to generate electricity or provide district heating. These systems are cheap and reduce the demand for non-renewable fossil fuels, which would themselves cause additional waste problems. A modern incineration plant is considered by many to be the safest method of waste disposal, but we could do more to reduce waste in the first place, and burning it is not the solution.

Into the water

Wastes dumped directly into water include waste water and material from industrial processes, sewage effluent, and ash from special incinerator ships. Other wastes find their way into the water system when they are absorbed by rainwater passing through soils, or as runoff from streets, fields, and buildings. Disposing waste into water was at one time thought to be safe, because it was assumed it would become harmless once it was diluted and

Outlet pipes dump treated and untreated wastes directly into the water. This pipe is dispensing untreated sewage into the North Sea.

spread over a wide area. It was also a popular option because it was cheaper and less visible than treating wastes on land.

However, population growth, industrial growth, and the greater use of chemicals in agriculture means that wastes are being pumped into water systems faster than nature can cope. It is now known that waste materials can build up in water to dangerous levels, causing damage to environments and to people. In the heavily developed European Union, 17 percent of coastal bathing areas failed to meet basic safety standards in 1996. Inland waters were even worse, with 70 percent falling below safe standards for recreational bathing.

Major rivers, such as the Rhine in Western Europe and the Ganges in India, are so polluted with industrial waste that they present a serious health hazard, and wildlife in some areas has completely disappeared. Some fishing communities have been affected by toxins entering the food chain and contaminating fish. The effect this could have on humans is made clear by the Japanese example of Minamata Bay, described in the next chapter.

Many countries have introduced strict regulations to control the dumping of wastes into water, and new technologies have reduced the volume of wastes produced in the first place. One success story is that of Long Island, where in 1991 people began to collect shellfish again after 30 years as a result of improved sewage treatment.

International waste trade
In the last 30 years, wealthier nations have exported waste across borders, because public awareness, environmental regulations, and land shortages have made disposal increasingly expensive at home, especially for hazardous wastes.

VIEWPOINTS

"In many cases, for non-combustible waste, the best disposal method may be landfilling."
Fred Pearce, New Scientist

"Britain has to stop chucking rubbish into landfill sites but plotting to cover Britain in new incinerators is no solution."
Mike Childs, Senior Waste Campaigner, Friends of the Earth

Some waste is so dangerous to human health that it can be handled only by waste experts wearing special protective clothing.

In the 1980s, for example, the average cost of hazardous waste disposal rose by 400 percent in Western Europe and by over 1,000 percent in the United States, leading many industries to look for cheaper options.

Most of this waste is now exported to developing countries where environmental laws are usually less strict and disposal costs are far cheaper. In Guinea, in West Africa, 15,000 tons of toxic ash from the United States were dumped at a cost of $40 per ton. This same waste would have cost at least $1,000 per ton to dump in the United States. Many developing countries have little choice but to accept such waste, since they need the money that this provides. Not all waste is exported to developing areas, however. Canada, for example, receives about 90 percent of U.S. hazardous waste exports, and Great Britain and France import used nuclear fuel from countries such as Japan and Germany.

In the late 1980s, the trade in hazardous waste was highlighted when a number of so-called "leper ships" were reported in the media to be sailing the oceans in search of a port for their toxic cargo. As knowledge spread around the world, they were rejected by country after country, and some ships, such as the *Karin B* from Italy, ended up back where they had started after over a year at sea.

VIEWPOINT

"Having relied for too long on the old strategy of 'out of sight, out of mind,' we are now running out of ways to dispose of our waste in a manner that keeps it out of either sight or mind."
U.S. Vice President Al Gore

Statistics for MSW (Municipal Solid Waste) Disposal Methods as Percent of Total (mid-1990s)

Country	Landfill	Incineration	Recycling/Composting
Japan	27	69	4
Korea	72	4	24
Denmark	22	54	24
Sweden	39	42	19
UK	84	9	7
Switzerland	14	46	40
United States	57	16	27
Mexico	99	0	1
Canada	75	6	19
Greece	93	0	7
France	59	32	9

Data from Organization for Economic Cooperation and Development (OECD)

DEBATE

No matter how hard we try to reduce waste, there will always be some items that have no further use. If you had to decide on the best disposal method for these, which would you choose and why?

THE COSTS OF WASTE

Who Pays for Waste?

If waste is managed carefully, then some say that it should not cause harm, but experience has shown that our wastes have damaged environments and in some cases caused great suffering, and even death, to humans. We can think of the effects of waste as "costs" that can be divided into three main types: environmental costs, human costs, and economic costs. They can also be considered at different levels, ranging from local costs, such as litter in the streets, to global costs, such as global warming.

Environmental costs

Nature is very good at looking after itself, but works only within certain limits. A number of different cycles ensure that wastes from one part of the environment become the raw materials for other parts. These cycles keep nature in balance, but human activity is threatening these, because it uses resources and produces wastes at a rate faster than nature can recycle them.

One global example is the buildup of atmospheric carbon dioxide as a result of our use of fossil fuels. Carbon dioxide occurs naturally, but human activity is disturbing natural cycles that are unable to absorb the extra quantity of carbon dioxide, resulting in what is known as the "greenhouse effect." This occurs when waste gases trap the heat of the sun's rays and warm up the Earth's atmosphere, in the same way that the glass of a greenhouse traps the air inside, making it warmer inside than out. The last 20 years of the twentieth century were the hottest ever recorded, which scientists say proves that the

Low-lying islands in the Pacific, like Hao atoll in French Polynesia, are threatened by rising sea levels caused by global warming.

greenhouse effect is heating the atmosphere in a process known as global warming. If temperatures continue to rise, scientists predict major changes to the world's weather patterns and rises in sea levels that could cause serious flooding in coastal areas and might even result in lowland areas and islands disappearing altogether.

In January 2000 Eastern Europe suffered serious environmental damage when over 3,531,448 cubic feet (100,000 m³) of cyanide leaked from a Romanian gold mine into the area's river network. The highly poisonous waste killed most of the life in the Tisza River, which flows through Romania and Hungary. It was responsible for fish deaths in the Danube River several hundred miles away, and it will be many years before life recovers in these rivers.

More localized environmental costs include the threat to Kenya's flamingo population around the town of Nakuru in the Great Rift Valley. Heavy metals from industrial waste discharged into Lake Nakuru have become concentrated over the years into levels that, by 1999, were killing thousands of birds that visited the lake to feed.

VIEWPOINT

The best estimate is that sea levels will have risen by around half a foot by the year 2100 and will continue to rise, even if greenhouse gas levels are stabilized.
World Health Organization (WHO) 1997

Hungarian fishermen collecting dead fish from the Tisza River following a leak of waste cyanide from the Aurul gold mine in Romania (January 2000)

Nature will often recover if given time, and cleaner technology and better regulations have led to improved environments in many countries. The Thames River in England now has otters and salmon living in parts of the river that were so polluted with industrial wastes in the 1950s that many thought wildlife would never return. However, environmentalists warn that we do not understand the long-term effects of wastes and should not rely on nature to clean them up. This is particularly true for the increasing number of new materials and chemicals that technological advances are allowing us to produce. Many of these, such as some plastics, may never degrade— and what about the radioactive waste that could still pose a danger in 250,000 years' time?

FACT

About two million seabirds die every year due to eating or becoming trapped in plastic waste.

Human costs

Several incidents around the world have demonstrated the potential harm of poor waste management to human health. One of the first reported incidents was at Minamata Bay in Japan in the 1950s. There, a local chemical factory was disposing of waste mercury by pumping it into the local water. The mercury settled on the ocean bed and was absorbed into the food chain, eventually contaminating fish that were a major part of the local people's diet. Residents began to suffer from nervous convulsions, blindness, and brain damage, which scientists later determined was caused by mercury poisoning from the local fish. The illness became known as "Minamata disease" and has been responsible for the deaths of over 300 people; a further 1,500 still suffer from symptoms today.

However, this is a small number compared to those who suffer and die every day from illnesses related to waste in many developing countries. An estimated four million people die every year from diseases such as diarrhea and dysentery related to water polluted with human waste. Development can reduce these deaths by providing basic facilities such as sanitation to dispose of human waste and a clean water supply to prevent contamination. In China only 24 percent of people have access to safe sanitation and 67 percent to safe water. In some of the poorest African countries, such as Malawi, the figures are even lower— only 3 percent have safe sanitation, and fewer than half have access to safe water. In most developed countries, these facilities are taken for granted, and it is easy to forget that these very basic waste problems kill more people than any of the modern industrial waste problems.

> **FACT**
>
> Each of us has about 500 synthetic chemicals in our bodies that were nonexistent before 1920.

Basic waste problems, such as polluted water, kill millions of people in developing countries. These Chinese women are cleaning clothes in the same water that people use to wash vegetables.

A health worker shows this Kenyan mother how to mix oral rehydration salts to treat diarrhea. Diarrhea kills millions of children every year and is normally caused by water contaminated with human sewage.

Why should people in developing areas be concerned about recycling paper, when they cannot even get safe water to drink?

A health problem shared throughout the world comes from wastes known as suspended particulate matter (SPM). These are the tiny particles of waste released into the air and visible as fumes, smoke, or dust. Suspended particulate matter often contain dangerous chemicals such as arsenic, benzene, cadmium, and lead. Lead particles emitted from gas engines are known to be particularly hazardous and can cause damage to the nervous system and harm children's brains. In 1975 the United States introduced lead-free gas. Many countries have since followed their example or at least reduced the amount of lead in their gas. The UK was one of the slower countries to act, and in 1988 only 1 percent of private vehicles used lead-free gas. It was only when taxes were introduced in 1989 to make leaded gas more expensive that unleaded gas use increased. Since 1999 leaded gas is no longer available in the UK, but in many developing countries it is still used and accounts for up to 95 percent of airborne lead, with levels twice those of most European countries.

VIEWPOINTS

"Particulate pollution affects more people globally on a continuing basis than any other pollutant."
WHO 1997

"Air pollution has been falling in modern industrialized countries for the last 40 years and it has been falling precisely because of economic growth and improvements in technology."
Steve Hayward, Director, Pacific Research Center

New technology has meant that air quality and health in many European and American cities has improved over the last 50 years, but in much of the developing world air pollution still causes major health problems. Industries and vehicles are normally older and less efficient, and laws controlling emissions of SPMs and other pollutants are less strict. Major cities in developing countries, such as Beijing, Bangkok, Cairo, and Mexico City, exceed acceptable levels of air pollution by up to 100 times.

The biggest source of SPMs in developing areas is smoke from the use of biomass fuels for cooking and heating. An estimated 2.5 million people die every year from diseases related to breathing, including bronchitis, tuberculosis, and heart disease. Many more suffer from irritating eye diseases that limit their ability to work and may even lead to blindness. Women and young children are particularly at risk

Pollution over Mexico City. The air in Mexico City is so bad that breathing it is equivalent to smoking 40 cigarettes a day—there are even oxygen dispensers that allow people to breathe clean air.

VIEWPOINTS

"...waste management must go beyond the mere safe disposal or recovery of wastes that are generated and seek to address the root cause of the problem by attempting to change unsustainable patterns of production and consumption."
United Nations Conference on Environment and Development 1992

"Those who benefit from economic growth are reluctant to give up their consumption patterns; those who aspire to one day achieving those patterns support development at any cost."
Rio de Janeiro Declaration

because they spend many hours cooking inside, where they are exposed to high levels of pollution. For these people modern fuels such as electricity or gas would improve their lives greatly, but these are expensive to develop, and relying on fossil fuels brings a different set of problems.

Economic costs

It is easy to forget that waste can have serious economic costs, like paying for people's health care or cleaning up damaged environments. Acid rain associated with fossil fuel emissions erodes buildings and poisons lakes and soils, killing fish and trees. All of these have an economic cost. However, reducing wastes can also mean significant costs, for which somebody has to pay. Because of this, many companies are slow to act in case people switch to buying cheaper products made by

Helicopters dump lime to neutralize acid rain damage in Scandinavian lakes. Such measures are very expensive.

companies that have not invested in new and cleaner technology. But companies that do invest in cleaner technology often find it actually saves money in the long run. In 1988 the Robbins Company in the United States introduced technology that reduced chemical use and wastes by almost 90 percent. It took only four years for the company to save money as a result of this investment.

Cleaning up the environment, such as this oil spill in Spain, can have far greater costs than taking greater care to avoid any damage in the first place.

Many experts now tell us that waste prevention is cheaper than dealing with the problems of waste, and the Minamata incident is a good example. In 1990 the costs of cleaning up the pollution at Minamata were over one hundred times more expensive than the waste prevention and control measures that would have avoided the problem in the first place.

In recent years the "Polluter Pays Principle" (PPP) has become popular, which argues that controlling waste should be paid for by those who produce it. An example of this is the tax introduced on leaded fuel in the UK, discussed earlier.

DEBATE

A school cafeteria has decided to look at ways to reduce waste. It is proposing to replace its disposable Styrofoam cups with glass mugs that can be washed after each use. From what you have learned so far about waste, which option do you think would have the lower costs?

REDUCTION, REUSE, AND RECOVERY

Think Before You Throw It?

Many scientists argue that improving the disposal of wastes is not enough. They suggest that we should instead minimize waste by following what they call a waste hierarchy. First, we should try to reduce waste, by improving technology and production processes and changing our consumption patterns. Secondly, we should think about how a product might be reused either for the same purpose or for a different use. If products cannot be reused, then we should recover the materials for alternative uses—this is often called recycling. Disposal of the product should be the last choice, and only made if the other options are not possible.

Curbside collection programs, like this one in California, provide people with special containers to separate their waste into different materials for recycling or safe disposal.

Waste reduction

Reducing levels of waste not only helps solve the problem of disposal, but also conserves resources for future generations—a major aim of sustainable development. Changes to manufacturing processes can be particularly effective, because industry and the extraction of raw materials are both major sources of waste. Improved technology means that many products can now be made thinner and lighter than they used to be—a process known as "lightweighting." For example, aluminum cans that weighed almost 4 ounces (100 g) in 1935 now weigh only .5 ounce (15 g).

New inventions, like the paper cartons now used for storing many foods and drinks, can also reduce wastes. They are lighter than alternative materials, such as glass, and are made mainly of renewable resources. Some are lined with a thin layer of aluminum, which protects foods labeled as "long life" without the need for refrigeration, and thus reducing energy consumption. But their greatest benefit is related to their transportation. Because they are manufactured flat, they are easier to transport to the factories where they are filled. One truck can deliver one million cartons, but an equal bottle capacity would need 26 trucks.

VIEWPOINT

"Unless plastic is compacted it is possible that more resources in the form of fuel may be burned in transporting the plastic than would be saved by recycling it."
East Sussex Recycling Consortium, UK

FACT

The movement of waste accounts for 15 percent of all freight transportation in France.

Garbage collectors in Jakarta, Indonesia, work with the local council to help reduce waste by collecting and selling items for reuse or recycling.

Reducing manufacturing wastes can also lower costs for the producer. In 1975 the Minnesota Mining and Manufacturing Corporation (3M) introduced changes that by 1989 had reduced air pollutants by 122,000 tons, solid wastes by 400,000 tons, and contaminated waste water by 1.8 billion gallons (7 billion l). These changes saved the company over $482 million. In 1996 the Kirin Brewery in Japan made annual savings of $9.5 million in transportation costs simply by reducing the weight of its beer bottles by 20 percent.

We can do simple things in our everyday lives to help reduce wastes. Buying loose fruit and vegetables rather than packaged ones, and buying in bulk instead of small amounts every week can reduce household rubbish considerably. Not flushing the toilet every time we use it, and saving laundry and plates until there is enough to clean a full load, can reduce our waste water emissions.

Reusing or repairing old products, like these computers in Hamburg, Germany, not only reduces waste but is also cheaper than buying new products.

A simple way to reduce waste is to use products such as clothes and electrical goods until the end of their useful lives, instead of throwing them away just because new fashions or models become available. Some companies have adopted this idea. Rank Xerox make remanufactured photocopiers by reusing the parts from old machines that are still in working order. This not only reduces waste, but has also saved the company millions of dollars and produces cheaper machines than their new ones.

It might be better to replace some products, however, especially if they are inefficient or polluting. Installing double-glazed windows reduces heat loss from buildings by up to 50 percent, and modern vehicles made of lighter materials and with catalytic converters produce fewer emissions and use less fuel than older models. Many modern washing machines use fewer than 18 gallons (70 l) of water and 1.3 kilowatts of electricity per wash compared to over 37 gallons (140 l) and 3.2 kilowatts for machines made in the 1970s.

More efficient forms of transportation, like this solar-powered Danish car called Mini-el, reduce waste emissions and use renewable resources—in this case the energy of the sun.

Reuse of waste

Products are often discarded with little thought, but many could be used again for the same purpose or for something different. Tires, for example, can be reused in many different ways. Car tires need to be replaced after about 35,000 miles (56,000 km), but they can be made to last much longer by adding new rubber to the worn surface in a process called re-treading. All airplane tires are re-treaded in this way to extend their life, but relatively few car tires are re-treaded, even though they are a cheaper option than buying new ones. Old tires are used as barriers at car racetracks to absorb the impact of vehicles and prevent drivers from injuring themselves if they crash. They are also tied to harbor walls to prevent boats from being damaged. Among their many other uses, old tires can be used for playground swings, or as weights to hold down silage covers on farms. They have even been filled with soil to make miniature gardens.

This Ugandan fisherman is reusing the reinforcing wire from old tires to make fishing baskets. The rubber from the tires is reused to make sandals.

Breaking up old tires in a process called granulation produces rubber crumb, which is used to make various products, including carpet underlay and car bumpers. It is also mixed with asphalt to make recreation surfaces for tennis courts and playgrounds, and trials are being conducted to see if it can be used to make road surfaces quieter. Despite these many reuses, 52 percent of the 300 million tires used each year in Europe are disposed of in landfill sites, but a new European law means this practice will be banned in 2006.

Some supermarkets now provide strong bags or boxes that are designed for customers to reuse each time they go shopping. Customers are normally asked to pay a small initial fee for the carriers, but this means that some people use the free disposable bags instead. However, even disposable bags may last several visits or be reused as liners for wastebaskets.

Products designed for reuse can actually be more wasteful in some situations. For example, glass beer bottles that are designed to be reused up to fifty times are thicker and heavier than a bottle designed for a single use. This means that if they are not reused, they are more wasteful of resources. It is also important to consider the wastes generated by the transportation and cleaning involved in reusing such products.

Waste recovery

Recycling is the best known form of waste recovery. Products like glass, aluminum, and paper are now regularly recycled by the public in many countries. People normally take goods to community collection points such as bottle banks, or sort their recyclable items into different materials for curbside collection.

Transporting waste for recycling can use a lot of energy and produce waste itself, such as exhaust fumes. Community recycling, like this boy collecting used bottles in Romania, are better.

VIEWPOINTS

"We need to use less paper and to recycle more of the paper we do use. The day-to-day demand for paper is putting immense pressure on the world's forests."
Friends of the Earth, Waste and Recycling *1999*

"If you value your environment, don't put this magazine in the paper bank once you have read it. The green option is to burn it."
Fred Pearce, New Scientist

FACT

Finland's forest is growing at a rate of 3 billion cubic feet (85 million m³) per year. This is 1.6 billion cubic feet (30 million m³) more than the depletion through logging and natural losses.

Recycling can save resources, lower costs, and reduce waste emissions, but not all products can be recovered in this way, and some materials are easier to recycle than others. Metals such as aluminum and steel can be recycled indefinitely without losing any strength or quality, and manufacturing using recovered metal uses much less energy and produces fewer emissions than when raw materials are used. In 1998 around 37 percent of aluminum cans were recycled in Europe compared to just 2 percent in 1989, but this still means that most were unnecessarily thrown away. In Brazil an estimated 100,000 people who earn their living by collecting aluminum cans helped Brazil to recycle 64 percent of them in 1997, which is one of the highest rates in the world.

Paper is another common product for recycling, but it deteriorates in quality and can only be recycled up to four times. This means that trees will always be needed for raw materials, but recycling can help to make trees a renewable resource by reducing deforestation and allowing time for planted trees to mature. Each ton of paper that is recycled saves around 15 average-sized trees and also protects local forest habitats.

Plastics are difficult to recycle, because there are many different types—it can be hard to tell them apart, and they cannot be mixed together. The problem of recycling plastics is made worse because they are often part of multimaterial products, such as the clear windows in paper envelopes or the casing for electrical goods.

There are some plastics that are easy to identify and recycle, such as PET (Polyethylene Terephthalate), a plastic used in making clear bottles for soft drinks. The plastic is heated until it melts and then is spun into special insulating fibers. These are used for

This Danish plant produces new cardboard products from recycled paper and cardboard waste. Because of the energy used in this process, some experts question the benefits of recycling.

making duvets, sleeping bags, and fleece jackets, one of which may contain the equivalent of 25 PET bottles. However, the light weight and high volume of PET bottles presents a problem, since 20,000 bottles are needed to make one ton of plastic. Most of the collection container is full of air, so a lot of transportation is needed to collect a relatively small number of bottles.

Some plastic goods, such as shopping bags, can have chemicals added during production that make them degrade when they are exposed to sunlight. This process is called photodegradation.

Artists use waste materials in many creative ways. This African drummer is made out of old exhaust pipes. Look for recycled arts and crafts in your local stores, or try it yourself.

In France photodegradable plastics are turned into a mulch, which is spread onto farmland. It helps to keep the soil moist and warm, allowing crops to be grown earlier in the year.

Composting is a form of recovery that involves separating biodegradable wastes such as vegetable peelings, tea leaves, and garden cuttings from other garbage. These are normally then placed in special composting bins or simply piled up outside and left to decompose. Community composting is practiced in many countries for people without gardens or the space to do this. Natural processes break down the waste in the same way that leaves decompose on the forest floor. At the end of the process, the remaining compost is rich in recycled nutrients and makes an excellent natural fertilizer. In an average American or European household, up to 35 percent of domestic waste is suitable for composting in this way, and in many developing countries over 70 percent.

Even wastes that have no further use and are not suitable for recycling can still be valuable for their energy content. Waste incineration can generate electricity or heat, which some say is an efficient method of waste disposal. In Canada and the UK less than 10 percent of MSW is handled in this way, but in Sweden the figure is around 55 percent and in Switzerland almost 90 percent. The leftover ash can be a useful resource for the construction industry—in Germany and Denmark it is used for path and road bases, and in the United States it is used to make cement building blocks. In Japan they are experimenting with "eco-cement," which is made of 50 percent ash from waste incinerators.

VIEWPOINT

"An end to the effluent society will lead to a more affluent society."
Norman Myers, The GAIA Atlas of Future Worlds

Energy consumption per use for 12-fluid ounce (350-ml) drink containers (including treatment but not transportation)

Container	Energy Use in kilojoules
Aluminum can, used once	7,500
Steel can, used once	6,300
Recycled steel can	4,100
Glass beer bottle, used once	3,900
Recycled aluminum can	2,700
Recycled glass beer bottle	2,700
Refillable glass bottle, used 10 times	640

Source: The State of New Zealand's Environment 1997

DEBATE

Pick something out of your wastebasket, and think about the wastes created during the life of that product. Is throwing it away still the best option? What could you do instead?

ACTION AND ATTITUDES

What Can Be Done?

Much of the technology that allows us to follow the three Rs (reduction, reuse, recovery) already exists, and many people say that it is the actions and attitudes of governments, companies, and the general public that must change.

Actions

Some large environmental groups, such as Greenpeace, have become world-famous for their direct actions, such as when their small inflatable boats tried to stop ships from dumping barrels of nuclear waste in the Atlantic Ocean. Today these groups have millions of members and can be very influential in persuading governments to introduce new regulations, or in their campaigns against companies that use damaging production techniques.

Public awareness of waste issues has become much greater, and demonstrations such as this one in Budapest, Hungary, are common in many countries.

Actions by local communities can be just as effective. The citizens' group organized by Lois Marie Gibbs eventually persuaded the American government to do something about toxic wastes leaking from Love Canal in the 1970s. You may have seen local groups taking action in the form of roadblocks, public rallies, or banners, that make others aware of the problems and try to force changes. Such local actions are often associated with something called NIMBY, which stands for "not in my backyard." This describes the people who may enjoy the benefits of modern living but do not want to see wastes stored or disposed of close to where they live. Some say that NIMBY is unfair, because if people enjoy the benefits of production and consumption, they should also share in the wastes it produces. In most developed countries, where NIMBY is a particular problem, the regulations for controlling waste have been greatly improved, and modern scientific instruments can alert the public to even the tiniest level of pollutants in the soil, water, or air before there is any danger.

Denmark plans to generate 20 percent of its electricity by wind power by 2007, but local residents do not want turbines, like these at Bonnerup, in their own backyards.

VIEWPOINT

"The big issue with wind power is the public acceptance in terms of visibility and noise."
Michael Graham, wind energy expert, Imperial College, London

International laws and agreements

International law has played an increasingly important part in waste and recycling, since it has been realized that many wastes can travel great distances. For example, many of the emissions that have caused acid rain damage in Scandinavian lakes and forests were blown there from the UK, and the emissions of greenhouse gases that are affecting the whole world come mainly from a small number of the most developed countries.

Since the 1970s several international agreements have been made to try and regulate the most damaging types of waste. In 1986, for example, a number of African countries demanded tighter controls on the international waste trade, after highly toxic waste had been dumped in their countries. An agreement called the Basel Convention was made in Switzerland in 1989 to try and regulate this trade by asking countries to prove that they could handle hazardous waste safely before it was traded. Despite this agreement hazardous waste is still traded, and some African countries will accept imports even if they cannot store them safely, because it earns them large sums of money. Companies in industrialized countries are happy to keep exporting such waste, since it is cheaper than disposing of it in their own country.

Air emissions have been the subject of two major international agreements. In 1987 the Montreal Protocol introduced a ban on the production of CFCs, the industrial gases that destroy the ozone layer. The ban came into effect in 1996, although developing countries were given until 2006 to find alternatives for their growing industries. The emission of other greenhouse gases, and especially carbon dioxide, was the subject of the United Nations Framework Convention on Climate Change agreed by over 150 countries at the 1992

VIEWPOINT

"We, as young people, have a particular interest in the future as we are destined to occupy it for longer than older people."
Rescue Mission Planet Earth

"The Tree of Life" became a symbol of hope for sustainable development when leaders met at the 1992 Earth Summit in Brazil. World leaders have since been criticized for their lack of action.

Earth Summit in Rio de Janeiro, Brazil. The agreement aimed to reduce emissions of carbon dioxide to lower than their 1990 levels by the year 2000, and in 1997 many countries signed agreements to reduce emissions further at a meeting in Kyoto, Japan.

Local laws and action

Some countries have introduced their own regulations to control waste: Germany introduced a law in 1991 to make companies responsible for the packaging from their products. Duales System Deutschland (DSD) was set up to collect, separate, and recycle packaging materials to help companies to meet these new regulations. France introduced a similar plan in 1993 aimed at recycling 75 percent of packaging waste by 2003, through the Eco-Emballages company.

In the UK the government introduced a landfill tax in 1996 to try and encourage the three Rs and divert waste away from landfill sites. This may seem to be a good idea, but some companies are now illegally dumping thousands of tons of waste in unregulated sites to avoid paying the tax. This is known as "fly-tipping," and there are several sites in the UK contaminated with highly toxic waste that will cost millions of dollars to clean up.

Attitudes

Many environmentalists believe that changing people's attitudes toward waste and recycling will bring greater changes than introducing laws. They argue that if people demand reusable or recyclable products that produce minimal waste then manufacturers will change their activities accordingly. This has been called "the power of the consumer," and in the late 1980s it led to a rush of "Green Consumerism" when it became very fashionable to buy environmentally friendly goods.

Today, products such as recycled paper, energy-efficient washing machines, phosphate-free washing powder, and recyclable packaging are all around us, but is simply buying these goods enough? In many cases no. People still throw away aluminum and steel cans instead of recycling them; they still drive short distances instead of walking or using public transportation; and many still want the latest fashion or the newest products when they already have usable items. For real changes in waste

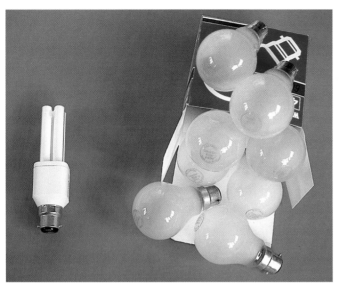

The energy-efficient lightbulb (shown left) lasts eight times longer than ordinary bulbs, so although it costs more to buy, it is much cheaper in the long run.

and recycling to occur, people's behavior must also change, but people are not easy to persuade, as the following Body Shop example shows. The Body Shop sells many of its cosmetic and personal care products in reusable plastic bottles and offers a 10 percent discount to customers who return them for refilling. Despite this service only 4 percent of customers returned their bottles in 1996, and most were simply thrown away.

This example suggests that people are perhaps too lazy to change their behavior, particularly in some wealthier countries. These have become known as "throw-away societies." In poorer countries goods such as shoes and radios are repaired instead of discarded, and many items are found alternative uses. Laziness can also affect recycling activities if people do not sort and clean goods properly. If you fail to put glass bottles into the correct colored containers, or leave metal lids on them, the whole batch may be rejected by the recycling plant. New technology often finds ways to cope with our laziness—in the United States, Brandt Technologies has developed a special coating to give glass its color instead of

FACT

If the three most used lightbulbs in every household were replaced with CFLs (compact fluorescent lamps), household emissions of carbon dioxide would be cut by 6.7 percent.

mixing color into clear glass when it is produced. The coating will melt when the glass is heated for recycling, so this removes the need for color sorting.

Many suggest that mountains of garbage like this will only be reduced when those of us living in "throw-away societies" change our own attitudes.

VIEWPOINTS

"Opinion polls suggest that the majority of people would prefer to live more sustainably, but do not have the skills, time, or resources to make the changes on their own."
Organization for Economic Cooperation and Development (OECD) 1997

"...many firms are still reluctant to implement a waste minimization program. A report by Biffa Waste Services suggested that 44 percent of companies do not even track waste costs and over half have no plans for waste minimization."
Friends of the Earth Briefing Sheet 1997 "Don't Burn or Bury It"

Recycled goods are sometimes considered poor quality, but they are normally as good as new products and often far cheaper because the materials cost less, or sometimes nothing at all. However some waste-reducing technology, such as energy- and resource-efficient goods, can be more expensive, which means that people must be prepared to pay for an improved environment. In reality these may end up cheaper in the long run, because they will cut down on bills and the use of resources, but many people only consider the immediate cost. Environmentalists encourage us to consider the full life cycle of a product and not just its immediate cost. Measures such as improved labeling to show how efficient a product is, or how it can be recycled, would help consumers to make better decisions.

Even with such help many people will still buy the cheaper or more fashionable product, which leads some to say that the polluter pays principle (PPP) is the only solution. Products would be priced according to their use and damage to resources, and companies making wasteful products would be forced to change. If this policy was adopted, however, industries in many developing countries might be unable to compete, because they cannot afford the latest clean technologies.

This woman collecting fuelwood in Nepal depends on her environment to survive, whereas tourists (like the one in the background) complain about the damage they cause. Who do you think causes more damage?

What is really needed is a combination of actions and attitudes. For example, regulations for environmental labeling would help us to change our attitudes about waste and recycling, but such regulations might not be introduced until we show a concern, so our actions are also important.

SUSTAINABLE FUTURES?

The Baygen clockwork radio is powered by winding it up, avoiding the wastes associated with batteries or electricity. It is a sustainable product that has been very successful.

Is It too Late?

The previous chapters have discussed some of the issues surrounding waste and recycling at the beginning of the 21st century. We have learned that unless we act soon to reduce our impact on the environment there is a risk of irreversible damage through effects such as global warming. But technology, as we have discovered, is finding solutions to many of our waste concerns, and in the most developed countries many are actually cleaner than they were 50 years ago. So what is the answer?

Sustainable development
In the late 1980s, a new idea was suggested—the idea of sustainable development. This view suggested that economic growth was necessary, but that it should be healthy growth that would not damage the environment or destroy resources for future generations. Today people talk about sustainable industries and sustainable housing; you can buy paper made from sustainable forest plantations and organic foods produced using sustainable farming methods. However, nearly all of our energy and many of our raw materials still come from nonrenewable sources that are not sustainable.

Models for the future
So what might a genuine sustainable future include? Energy would come from renewable resources such as the sun or the wind. Solar energy is already in everyday use to power items such as calculators and watches, but it is rarely used for larger demands and in 1990 supplied only 0.1 percent of world energy.

Wind generation supplies even less, but increased by about 20 percent in 1996 alone and is expected to grow rapidly in the future. In India it is estimated that by 2030 up to 25 percent of energy could be generated by the wind.

Industries will need to copy natural cycles and cooperate more if they are to be sustainable. In the Danish city of Kalundborg, seven industrial plants and thousands of farmers and residents exchange an estimated three million tons of material each year that would previously have been treated as waste. In Brazil, alcohol produced from sugarcane plantations is used to fuel vehicles instead of gasoline, reducing pollution considerably.

Organic agriculture will need to replace existing practices that rely on large quantities of chemicals (fertilizers and pesticides). The demand for organic food is growing rapidly as people become aware of the damage that chemicals can cause in the environment. In Japan, over three million people now buy organic food, and worldwide sales are expected to increase from $11 billion in 1997 to $100 billion by 2006. Farming organically does not necessarily mean lower production as critics suggest. In Indonesia, rice farmers reduced their pesticide use by 65 percent while increasing production by 12 percent.

This home in southern India uses solar panels on its roof to heat its water. Many believe that we will have to follow this example if we are to have a sustainable future.

This plant in Iceland uses the natural heat from deep under the Earth's surface to generate electricity. This is a renewable form of energy called geothermal power.

VIEWPOINTS

"Increases in pollution stimulate the development of better, cleaner technology, and new methods of cleaning up the mess."
Matthew Lockwood in "An Overcrowded World" 1995

"Science and technology possess enormous potential to assist in caring for the Earth, but they must be employed in a careful, balanced, and responsible way. The 'technical fix' approach is neither balanced nor sustainable."
John Houghton, Global Warming

Participation

A sustainable future will depend on people becoming involved in conserving and using resources efficiently, and there are many things we can do to help. We can follow the three Rs and help others to understand the potential problems of waste and the alternative options to simply throwing things away. In Ghana, children as young as 12 have organized cleanup campaigns to remove waste from community areas, and in Kampala, Uganda, young people have set up composting programs to help keep their communities clean.

The 1992 Earth Summit saw the launch of Agenda 21, a set of guidelines to advise governments and local councils how to achieve sustainable development. One aim is to encourage citizens to become involved in sustainable development by thinking globally but acting locally. However,

58

governments have been criticized for not informing people about Agenda 21 and what they can do in their community. Try and find out what your local council is doing about Agenda 21.

Enough is enough?

No matter what governments and industries do, a sustainable future will depend on people like you and me making our own decisions. You may decide that technology will solve our waste problems, or maybe, like many environmentalists, you think we have already done too much damage. With so much debate about waste and recycling it is difficult to know what to do for the best. Do we continue to take risks with the future, or is it time to say enough is enough and act now? Now that you know more about the issues involved it is really up to you!

Technology such as the Internet, being used here at a café in Taipei, Taiwan, can reduce waste by reducing our need to travel and the amount of paper we use.

DEBATE

Think about all the changes that you and your family could make to be more sustainable. Now think about how easy or difficult it would be actually to make those changes. What does this tell you about our chances for a sustainable future?

GLOSSARY

biodegradable able to be broken down and recycled naturally, through the action of the weather and other living things (plants, animals, bacteria, etc.).

biomass fuels natural fuels that use plant or animal waste. They include wood, crop stalks, animal dung, and collected leaves. They are normally dried and burned, but animal dung can be used to produce a type of gas called biogas.

carcinogenic a substance that increases the risk of cancer when humans are exposed to it.

CFCs the abbreviation for a group of chemicals called chlorofluorocarbons that destroy ozone in the atmosphere for up to 100 years after they are released. They can be found in refrigerators, fire extinguishers, and some aerosol sprays. Today their use is banned in new products.

DDT the abbreviation for Dichloro-Diphenyl-Trichloroethane, an insecticide used to kill mosquitoes. But it has harmful side effects on people, animals, and fish. It is now banned in many countries but still used in some developing countries.

developed countries the wealthier countries of the world including North America, Europe, Japan, Australia, and New Zealand.

developing countries the poorer countries of the world, sometimes called the Third World, and including most of Africa, Asia, and Latin America.

dioxins highly toxic chemical wastes produced during the manufacture or disposal of products such as electrical goods and herbicides for controlling weeds. Dioxins can also be produced when incinerators do not fully burn plastic waste.

ecosystem the contents of an environment, including all the plants and animals that live there. This could be a garden pond, a forest, or the whole Earth.

effluent liquid wastes that are either stored or discharged directly into streams, lakes, or the oceans. Mining, industrial processes, and sewage treatment all produce large quantities of effluent.

emissions waste products (normally gases and solid particles) released into the atmosphere. These include car exhaust fumes and the wastes from chimneys at power plants and factories.

food chain the transfer of energy from producers (algae, plants, etc.) to consumers (animals and humans) as organisms feed on one another.

fossil fuels term to describe energy sources such as coal, oil, and gas formed millions of years ago by the fossilized remains of plants and animals.

global warming the gradual warming of the Earth's atmosphere as a result of greenhouse gases trapping heat. Human activity has increased the level of greenhouse gases, such as carbon dioxide and methane, in the atmosphere.

greenhouse gas an atmospheric gas that traps some of the heat radiating from the Earth's surface.

Industrial Revolution
the period in the late 18th century and early 19th century (150 to 250 years ago) when new machinery and the use of fossil fuels to generate energy led to the start of modern industry, and dramatic changes in the way people lived.

leachate a liquid that is formed when rainwater enters a landfill site and carries diluted chemicals and metals with it as it passes through the garbage. If it is not contained, the leachate can enter streams and pollute local water and land.

life cycle the whole life of a product, including the energy used in transporting or transforming the product into something else. It is used by scientists to measure the different impact products have on the environment.

organic a product of living organisms that occurs naturally in the environment. Organic substances can be broken down by nature—they are biodegradable.

PCBs the abbreviation for a group of chemicals called polychlorinated biphenyls used in electrical goods and some plastics. PCBs release dioxins if not properly disposed of in incinerators at over 2,190°F (1,200 °C).

remanufacture a process where waste from manufactured goods becomes a resource for manufacturing a different product. For example, plastic drink bottles can be melted to make fleece jackets.

renewable resources resources that are easily replaced or replace themselves to be used again.

The sun is a renewable energy resource because it can be reused every day, but coal or oil that takes millions of years to replace itself is not.

sewage waste carried by sewers for treatment or disposal. Sewage normally includes human wastes and waste water, but can include chemicals from homes, offices, and factories.

slurry a liquid containing a large quantity of solid material, normally like a thick paste. Slurry is a common waste from mining operations, and of farmyards as diluted animal wastes.

synthetic an artificial substance manufactured or created by using natural resources.

BOOKS TO READ

Chandler, Gary, and Kevin Graham. *Recycling*. Twenty-First Century, 1996.

Gore, Al. *Earth in the Balance: Ecology and the Human Spirit*. Plume, reprint edition, 1993.

Parker, Steve. *Waste, Recycling, and Reuse*. Raintree Steck-Vaughn, 1998.

Roleff, Tamara L. *Global Warming: Opposing Viewpoints*. Greenhaven, 1997.

Woods, Samuel G. *Recycled Paper: From Start to Finish*. Blackbirch, 2000.

USEFUL ADDRESSES

http://www.epa.gov/students
The student pages of the United States Environmental Protection Agency provide information, facts, and data on environmental issues, including waste and recycling.

http://www.war-on-waste.com
This South African site specializes in educational materials looking at paper recycling. It also has some useful resources, fun activities, and related links.

http://www.greenpeace.org
The website for the environmental action group Greenpeace. It contains news and information about current and past debates as well as useful links to other organizations.

http://www.foe.org
The Friends of the Earth site provides information about current environmental campaigns as well as links to other useful sites. It has regular features on waste and recycling.

UNITED STATES

Friends of the Earth
1025 Vermont Avenue, N.W.
Washington, DC 20005
Tel: (292) 783-7400

Greenpeace
702 H Street, N.W., Suite 300
Washington, DC 20001
Tel: (202) 452-1177

U.S. Environmental Protection Agency
Ariel Rios Building
1200 Pennsylvania Avenue, N.W.
Washington, DC 20460
Tel: (202) 260-2090

CANADA

Greenpeace
250 Dundas Street West, Suite 605
Toronto, Ontario
Canada M5T 2Z5
Tel: 416-597-8408
    1-800-320-7183
Fax: 416-597-8422
www.greenpeacecanada.org

INDEX

INDEX